THE
DIVING BELL
AND THE
BUTTERFLY

JEAN-DOMINIQUE BAUBY

THE
DIVING BELL
AND THE
BUTTERFLY

WHEELER
PUBLISHING, INC.
ROCKLAND, MA

★ AN AMERICAN COMPANY ★

Copyright © 1997 by Editions Robert Laffont, S.A., Paris

Published in Large Print by arrangement with Alfred A. Knopf, Inc. in the United States and Canada.

Wheeler Large Print Book Series.

Set in 16 pt Plantin.

Library of Congress Cataloging-in-Publication Data

Bauby, Jean-Dominique.
   [Scaphandre et le papillon. English]
       p. (large print) cm.(Wheeler large print book series)
   ISBN 1-56895-496-4 (hardcover)
   1. Bauby, Jean–Dominique—Health. 2. Cerebrovascular disease—
Patients—France—Biography. 3. Periodical editors—France—Biography.
4. Large type books.
I. Title. II. Series
[RC388.5.B39513 1997b]
362.1'9681—dc21
[B]   97-34582
                                                                CIP

For my children, Théophile and Céleste...

*And my deepest gratitude to Claude Mendibil,
whose all-important contribution to these pages
will become clear as my story unfolds*

CONTENTS

THE
DIVING BELL
AND THE
BUTTERFLY

Prologue

Through the frayed curtain at my window, a wan glow announces the break of day. My heels hurt, my head weighs a ton, and something like a giant invisible diving bell holds my whole body prisoner. My room emerges slowly from the gloom. I linger over every item: photos of loved ones, my children's drawings, posters, the little tin cyclist sent by a friend the day before the Paris–Roubaix bike race, and the IV pole hanging over the bed where I have been confined these past six months, like a hermit crab dug into his rock.

No need to wonder very long where I am, or to recall that the life I once knew was snuffed out Friday, the eighth of December, last year.

Up until then, I had never even heard of the brain stem. I've since learned that it is an essential component of our internal computer, the inseparable link between the brain and the spinal cord. I was brutally introduced to this vital piece of anatomy when a cerebrovascular accident took my brain stem out of action. In the past, it was known as a "massive stroke," and you simply died. But improved resuscitation

1

techniques have now prolonged and refined the agony. You survive, but you survive with what is so aptly known as "locked-in syndrome." Paralyzed from head to toe, the patient, his mind intact, is imprisoned inside his own body, unable to speak or move. In my case, blinking my left eyelid is my only means of communication.

Of course, the party chiefly concerned is the last to hear the good news. I myself had twenty days of deep coma and several weeks of grogginess and somnolence before I truly appreciated the extent of the damage. I did not fully awake until the end of January. When I finally surfaced, I was in Room 119 of the Naval Hospital at Berck-sur-Mer, on the French Channel coast—the same Room 119, infused now with the first light of day, from which I write.

An ordinary day. At seven the chapel bells begin again to punctuate the passage of time, quarter hour by quarter hour. After their night's respite, my congested bronchial tubes once more begin their noisy rattle. My hands, lying curled on the yellow sheets, are hurting, although I can't tell if they are burning hot or ice cold. To fight off stiffness, I instinctively stretch, my arms and legs moving only a fraction of an inch. It is often enough to bring relief to a painful limb.

My diving bell becomes less oppressive, and my mind takes flight like a butterfly.

There is so much to do. You can wander off in space or in time, set out for Tierra del Fuego or for King Midas's court.

You can visit the woman you love, slide down beside her and stroke her still-sleeping face. You can build castles in Spain, steal the Golden Fleece, discover Atlantis, realize your childhood dreams and adult ambitions.

Enough rambling. My main task now is to compose the first of these bedridden travel notes so that I shall be ready when my publisher's emissary arrives to take my dictation, letter by letter. In my head I churn over every sentence ten times, delete a word, add an adjective, and learn my text by heart, paragraph by paragraph.

Seven-thirty. The duty nurse interrupts the flow of my thoughts. Following a well-established ritual, she draws the curtain, checks tracheostomy and drip feed, and turns on the TV so I can watch the news. Right now a cartoon celebrates the adventures of the fastest frog in the West. And what if I asked to be changed into a frog? What then?

The Wheelchair

I had never seen so many white coats in my little room. Nurses, orderlies, physical therapist, occupational therapist, psychologist, neurologist, interns, and even the department head—the whole hospital had turned out for the event. When they first burst in, pushing the conveyance ahead of them, I thought it meant that I was being ejected to make room for a new patient. I had already been at Berck a few weeks and was daily drawing nearer to the shores of awareness, but I still could not imagine any connection between a wheelchair and me.

No one had yet given me an accurate picture of my situation, and I clung to the certainty, based on bits and pieces I had overheard, that I would very quickly recover movement and speech.

Indeed, my roving mind was busy with a thousand projects: a novel, travel, a play, marketing a fruit cocktail of my own invention. (Don't ask for the recipe; I have forgotten it.) They immediately dressed me. "Good for the morale," pronounced the neurologist in sententious tones. And in truth I would have

5

been pleased to trade my yellow nylon hospital gown for a plaid shirt, old pants, and a shapeless sweater—except that it was a nightmare to put them on. Or rather to watch the clothes manipulated, after endless contortions, over these uncooperative deadweight limbs, which serve me only as a source of pain.

When I was finally dressed, the ritual could begin. Two attendants seized me by the shoulders and feet, lifted me off the bed, and dumped me unceremoniously into the wheelchair. I had graduated from being a patient whose prognosis was uncertain to an official quadriplegic. They didn't quite applaud, but they came close. My caretakers made me travel the length and breadth of the hospital floor, to make certain that the seated position did not trigger uncontrollable spasms, but I was too devastated by this brutal downgrading of my future hopes to take much notice. They had to place a special cushion behind my head: it was wobbling about like the head of one of those African women upon removal of the stack of rings that has been stretching her neck for years. "You can handle the wheelchair," said the occupational therapist, with a smile intended to make the remark sound like good news, whereas to my ears it had the ring of a life sentence. In one flash I saw the frightening truth. It was as blinding as an atomic explosion and keener than a guillotine blade. They all left.

As three orderlies laid me back down, I thought of movie gangsters struggling to fit the slain informer's body into the trunk of their car. The wheelchair sat abandoned in a corner, with my clothes tossed over its dark-blue plastic backrest. Before the last white coat left the room, I signaled my wish to have the TV turned on, low. On the screen was my father's favorite quiz show. Since daybreak, an unremitting drizzle had been streaking my windows.

Prayer

Oddly enough, the shock of the wheelchair was helpful. Things became clearer. I gave up my grandiose plans, and the friends who had built a barrier of affection around me since my catastrophe were able to talk freely. With the subject no longer taboo, we began to discuss locked-in syndrome. First of all, it is very rare. It is small consolation, but the chances of being caught in this hellish trap are about as likely as those of winning the lottery. At Berck, only two of us were locked in, and my own case was not classic. I am able to swivel my head, which is not supposed to be part of the clinical picture. Since most victims are relegated to a vegetable existence, the evolution of the disease is not well understood. All that is known is that if the nervous system makes up its mind to start working again, it does so at the speed of a hair growing from the base of the brain. So it is likely that several years will go by before I can expect to wiggle my toes.

In fact, it is in my respiratory passages that I can hope for improvement. In the long term, I can hope to eat more normally: that is, without the help of a gastric tube. Eventually, perhaps I will be able to breathe naturally, without a respirator, and muster enough breath to make my vocal cords vibrate.

But for now, I would be the happiest of men if I could just swallow the overflow of saliva that endlessly floods my mouth. Even before first light, I am already practicing sliding my tongue toward the rear of my palate in order to provoke a swallowing reaction. What is more, I have dedicated to my larynx the little packets of incense hanging on the wall, amulets brought back from Japan by pious globe-trotting friends. Just one of the stones in the thanksgiving monument erected by my circle of friends during their wanderings. In every corner of the world, the most diverse deities have been solicited in my name. I try to organize all this spiritual energy. If they tell me that candles have been burned for my sake in a Breton chapel, or that a mantra has been chanted in a Nepalese temple, I at once give each of the spirits invoked a precise task. A woman I know enlisted a Cameroon holy man to procure me the goodwill of Africa's gods: I have assigned him my right eye. For my hearing problems I rely on the relationship between my devout mother-in-law and the monks of a Bordeaux brotherhood. They regularly dedicate their prayers to me, and I occasionally steal into their abbey to hear their chants fly heavenward. So far the results have been unremarkable. But when seven brothers of the same order had their throats cut by Islamic fanatics, my ears hurt for several days. Yet all these lofty protections are merely clay ramparts, walls of sand, Maginot lines, compared to the small prayer my daughter, Céleste, sends up to her Lord every evening before she closes her eyes. Since we fall asleep at roughly the same hour, I set out for the kingdom of slumber with this wonderful talisman, which shields me from all harm.

Bathtime

At eight-thirty the physical therapist arrives. Brigitte, a woman with an athletic figure and an imperial Roman profile, has come to exercise my stiffened arms and legs. They call the exercise "mobilization," a term whose martial connotations contrast ludicrously with the paltry forces thus summoned, for I've lost sixty-six pounds in just twenty weeks. When I began a diet a week before my stroke, I never dreamed of such a dramatic result. As she works, Brigitte checks for the smallest flicker of improvement. "Try to squeeze my hand," she asks. Since I sometimes have the illusion that I am moving my fingers, I focus my energy on crushing her knuckles, but nothing stirs and she replaces my inert hand on its foam pad. In fact, the only sign of change is in my neck. I can now turn my head ninety degrees, and my field of vision extends from the slate roof of the building next door to the curious tongue-lolling Mickey Mouse drawn by my son, Théophile, when I was still unable to open my mouth. Now, after regular exercise, we have reached the stage of slipping a lollipop into it. As the neurologist says,

"We need to be very patient." The session with Brigitte ends with a facial massage. Her warm fingers travel all over my face, including the numb zone, which seems to me to have the texture of parchment, and the area that still has feeling, where I can manage the beginnings of a frown. Since the demarcation line runs across my mouth, I can only half-smile, which fairly faithfully reflects my ups and downs. A domestic event as commonplace as washing can trigger the most varied emotions.

One day, for example, I can find it amusing, in my forty-fifth year, to be cleaned up and turned over, to have my bottom wiped and swaddled like a newborn's. I even derive a guilty pleasure from this total lapse into infancy. But the next day, the same procedure seems to me un-bearably sad, and a tear rolls down through the lather a nurse's aide spreads over my cheeks. And my weekly bath plunges me simultaneously into distress and happiness. The delectable moment when I sink into the tub is quickly followed by nostalgia for the protracted immersions that were the joy of my previous life. Armed with a cup of tea or a Scotch, a good book or a pile of newspapers, I would soak for hours, maneuvering the taps with my toes. Rarely do I feel my condition so cruelly as when I am recalling such pleasures. Luckily I have no time for gloomy thoughts. Already they are wheeling me back, shivering, to my room, on a gurney as comfortable as a bed of nails.

I must be fully dressed by ten-thirty and ready to go to the rehabilitation center. Having turned down the hideous jogging suit provided by the hospital, I am now attired as I was in my student days. Like the bath, my old clothes could easily bring back poignant, painful memories. But I see in the clothing a symbol of continuing life. And proof that I still want to be myself. If I must drool, I may as well drool on cashmere.

The Alphabet

I am fond of my alphabet letters. At night, when it is a little too dark and the only sign of life is the small red spot in the center of the television screen, vowels and consonants dance for me to a Charles Trenet tune: "Dear Venice, sweet Venice, I'll always remember you..." Hand in hand, the letters cross the room, whirl around the bed, sweep past the window, wriggle across the wall, swoop to the door, and return to begin again.

E S A R I N T U L O M D P C F B
V H G J Q Z Y X K W

The jumbled appearance of my chorus line stems not from chance but from cunning calculation. More than an alphabet, it is a hit parade in which each letter is placed according to the frequency of its use in the French language. That is why E dances proudly out in front, while W labors to hold on to last place. B resents being pushed back next to V, and haughty J—which begins so many sentences in French—is amazed to find itself so near the rear of the pack. Roly-poly G is annoyed to have to

17

trade places with H, while T and U, the tender components of *tu,* rejoice that they have not been separated. All this reshuffling has a purpose: to make it easier for those who wish to communicate with me.

It is a simple enough system. You read off the alphabet (ESA version, not ABC) until, with a blink of my eye, I stop you at the letter to be noted. The maneuver is repeated for the letters that follow, so that fairly soon you have a whole word, and then fragments of more or less intelligible sentences. That, at least, is the theory. In reality, all does not go well for some visitors. Because of nervousness, impatience, or obtuseness, performances vary in the handling of the code (which is what we call this method of transcribing my thoughts). Crossword fans and Scrabble players have a head start. Girls manage better than boys. By dint of practice, some of them know the code by heart and no longer even turn to our special notebook—the one containing the order of the letters and in which all my words are set down like the Delphic oracle's.

Indeed, I wonder what conclusions anthropologists of the year 3000 will reach if they ever chance to leaf through these notebooks, where haphazardly scribbled remarks like "The physical therapist is pregnant," "Mainly on the legs," "Arthur Rimbaud," and "The French team played like pigs" are interspersed with unintelligible gibberish, misspelled words, lost letters, omitted syllables.

Nervous visitors come most quickly to grief. They reel off the alphabet tonelessly, at top speed, jotting down letters almost at random; and then, seeing the meaningless result, exclaim, "I'm an idiot!" But in the final analysis, their anxiety gives me a chance to rest, for they take charge of the whole conversation, providing both questions and answers, and I am spared the task of holding up my end. Reticent people are much more difficult. If I ask them, "How are you?" they answer, "Fine," immediately putting the ball back in my court. With some, the alphabet becomes an artillery barrage, and I need to have two or three questions ready in advance in order not to be swamped. Meticulous people never go wrong: they scrupulously note down each letter and never seek to unravel the mystery of a sentence before it is complete. Nor would they dream of completing a single word for you. Unwilling to chance the smallest error, they will never take it upon themselves to provide the "room" that follows "mush," the "ic" that follows "atom," or the "nable" without which neither "intermi" nor "abomi" can exist. Such scrupulousness makes for laborious progress, but at least you avoid the misunderstandings in which impulsive visitors bog down when they neglect to verify their intuitions. Yet I understood the poetry of such mind games one day when, attempting to ask for my glasses (*lunettes*), I was asked what I wanted to do with the moon (*lune*).

The Empress

Not many places in France still pay homage to Empress Eugénie. In the main hall of the Naval Hospital, a vast echoing space in which gurneys and wheelchairs can advance five abreast, a stained-glass window depicts the wife of Napoléon III, the hospital's patroness. The two chief curiosities of this mini-museum are a white marble bust, which restores her to the glory of her youth, and the letter in which the deputy stationmaster of Berck's railroad depot describes to the editor of the *Correspondant Maritime* the brief imperial visit of May 4, 1864. Through his words we clearly see the special train pull in carrying the troupe of young ladies of Eugénie's retinue, the joyful procession through the town, and the introduction of the hospital's little patients (Berck began life as a children's hospital) to their illustrious protectress. For a while I seized every chance I had to pay my respects to these relics.

A score of times I read the railwayman's account. I mingled with the chattering flock of ladies-in-waiting, and whenever Eugénie progressed from one ward to another, I followed her hat with its yellow ribbons, her silk parasol, and the scent of her passage, imbued with the eau de cologne of the court perfumer. On one particularly windy day, I even dared to draw near and bury my face in the folds of her white gauzy dress with its broad satin stripes. It was as sweet as whipped cream, as cool as the morning dew. She did not send me away. She ran her fingers through my hair and said gently, "There, there, my child, you must be very patient," in a Spanish accent very like the neurologist's. She was no longer the empress of the French but a compassionate divinity in the manner of Saint Rita, patroness of lost causes.

And then one afternoon as I confided my woes to her likeness, an unknown face interposed itself between us. Reflected in the glass I saw the head of a man who seemed to have emerged from a vat of formaldehyde. His mouth was twisted, his nose damaged, his hair tousled, his gaze full of fear. One eye was sewn shut, the other goggled like the doomed eye of Cain. For a moment I stared at that dilated pupil, before I realized it was only mine.

Whereupon a strange euphoria came over me. Not only was I exiled, paralyzed, mute, half deaf, deprived of all pleasures, and reduced to the existence of a jellyfish, but I was also horrible to behold. There comes a time when the heaping up of calamities brings on uncontrollable nervous laughter—when, after a final blow from fate, we decide to treat it all as a joke. My jovial cackling at first disconcerted Eugénie, until she herself was infected by my mirth. We laughed until we cried. The municipal band then struck up a waltz, and I was so merry that I would willingly have risen and invited Eugénie to dance, had such a move been fitting. We would have whirled around miles of floor. Ever since then, whenever I go through the main hall, I detect a hint of amusement in the empress's smile.

Cinecittà

The Naval Hospital must be a striking sight to the noisy light aircraft that buzz across the Berck shoreline at an altitude of three hundred feet. With its massive, overelaborate silhouette and the high redbrick walls typical of northern France, it seems to have foundered on the sands between the town and the gray waters of the Channel. On the facade of its most imposing annex, as on the front of schools and public baths in the French capital, are the words "City of Paris." Created during the Second Empire for sick children in need of a climate healthier than that of Paris's hospitals, the annex has retained its extraterritorial status.

For while cold reality places us in the Pas de Calais region, as far as the medical bureaucracy is concerned we are still on the banks of the Seine.

Linked by endless corridors, the hospital buildings form an authentic maze, and one routinely runs into patients from Ménard hopelessly lost in Sorrel—wards named after eminent surgeons. Like children who have wandered from their mothers, these unfortunates mutter "I'm lost!" as they wobble about on their crutches. Being what the stretcher bearers call a "Sorrel," I am more or less at home here, but the same cannot be said of newcomers. I could try to signal with my eyes whenever my wheelchair is pushed in the wrong direction, but I have taken to looking stonily ahead. There is always the chance that we will stumble upon some unknown corner of the hospital, see new faces, or catch a whiff of cooking as we pass. It was in this way that I came upon the lighthouse, on one of my very first expeditions in my wheelchair, shortly after swimming up from the mists of coma. As we emerged from an elevator on the wrong floor, I saw it: tall, robust, and reassuring, in red and white stripes that reminded me of a rugby shirt. I placed myself at once under the protection of this brotherly symbol, guardian not just of sailors but of the sick—those castaways on the shores of loneliness.

The lighthouse and I remain in constant touch, and I often call on it by having myself wheeled to Cinecittà, a region essential to my imaginary geography of the hospital. Cinecittà is the perpetually deserted terrace of Sorrel ward. Facing south, its vast balconies open onto a landscape heavy with the poetic and slightly offbeat charm of a movie set. The suburbs of Berck look like a model-train layout. A handful of buildings at the foot of the sand dunes gives the illusion of a Western ghost town. As for the sea, it foams such an incandescent white that it might be the product of the special-effects department.

I could spend whole days at Cinecittà. There, I am the greatest director of all time. On the town side, I reshoot the close-ups for *Touch of Evil.* Down at the beach, I rework the dolly shots for *Stagecoach,* and offshore I re-create the storm rocking the smugglers of *Moonfleet.* Or else I dissolve into the landscape and there is nothing more to connect me to the world than a friendly hand stroking my numb fingers. I am the hero of Godard's *Pierrot le Fou,* my face smeared blue, a garland of dynamite sticks encircling my head. The temptation to strike a match drifts by, like a cloud. And then it is dusk, when the last train sets out for Paris, when I have to return to my room. I wait for winter. Warmly wrapped up, we can linger here until nightfall, watch the sun set and the lighthouse take up the torch, its hope-filled beams sweeping the horizon.

Tourists

After devoting itself to the care of young victims of a tuberculosis epidemic after the Second World War, Berck gradually shifted its focus away from children. Nowadays it tends to concentrate more on the sufferings of the aged, on the inevitable breakdown of body and mind; but geriatrics is only one part of the picture I must paint to give an accurate idea of the hospital's denizens. In one section are a score of comatose patients, patients at death's door, plunged into endless night. They never leave their rooms. Yet everyone knows they are there, and they weigh strangely on our collective awareness, almost like a guilty conscience. In another wing, next door to the colony of elderly and enfeebled, is a cluster of morbidly obese patients whose substantial dimensions the doctors hope to whittle down. Elsewhere, a battalion of cripples forms the bulk of the inmates. Survivors of sport, of the highway, and of every possible and imaginable kind of domestic accident, these patients remain at Berck for as long as it takes to get their shattered limbs working again. I call them "tourists."

And to complete the picture, a niche must be found for us, broken-winged birds, voiceless parrots, ravens of doom, who have made our nest in a dead-end corridor of the neurology department. Of course, we spoil the view. I am all too conscious of the slight uneasiness we cause as, rigid and mute, we make our way through a group of more fortunate patients.

The best place to observe this phenomenon is the rehabilitation room, where all patients undergoing physical therapy are congregated. Garish and noisy, a hubbub of splints, artificial limbs, and harnesses of varying complexity, it is an authentic Court of Miracles. Here we see a young man with an earring who suffered multiple fractures in a motorbike accident; a grandmother in a fluorescent nightgown learning to walk after a fall from a stepladder; and a vagrant whose foot was somehow amputated by a subway train. Lined up like a row of onions, this human throng waves arms and legs under minimal supervision, while I lie tethered to an inclined board that is slowly raised to a vertical position. Every morning I spend half an hour suspended this way, frozen to attention in a posture that must evoke the appearance of the Commendatore's statue in the second act of Mozart's *Don Giovanni*. Below, people laugh, joke, call out. I would like to be part of all this hilarity, but as soon as I direct my one eye toward them, the young man, the grandmother, and the homeless man turn away, feeling the sudden need to study the ceiling smoke detector. The "tourists" must be very worried about fire.

The Sausage

After every day's session on the vertical board, a stretcher bearer wheels me from the rehabilitation room and parks me next to my bed, where I wait for the nurse's aides to swing me back between the sheets. And every day, since by now it is noon, the same stretcher bearer wishes me a resolutely cheerful *"Bon appetit!"*—his way of saying "See you tomorrow." And of course, to wish me a hearty appetite is about the same as saying "Merry Christmas" on August 15 or "Good night" in broad daylight. In the last eight months I have swallowed nothing save a few drops of lemon-flavored water and a half teaspoon of yogurt, which gurgled noisily down my windpipe. The feeding test—as they grandly called this banquet—was not a success. But no call for alarm: I haven't starved. By means of a tube threaded into my stomach, two or three bags of a brownish fluid provide my daily caloric needs. For pleasure, I have to turn to the vivid memory of tastes and smells, an inexhaustible reservoir of sensations. Once, I was a master at recycling leftovers. Now I cultivate the art of simmering memories. You can sit down to a meal at any hour, with no fuss or ceremony. If it's a restaurant, no need to call ahead. If I do the cooking, it is always a success. The *bœuf bourguignon* is tender, the *bœuf en gelée* translucent, the apricot pie possesses just the requisite tartness. Depending on my mood, I treat myself to a dozen snails, a plate of Alsatian sausage with sauerkraut, and a bottle of late-vintage golden Gewürztraminer; or else I savor a simple soft-boiled egg with fingers of toast and lightly salted butter. What a banquet! The yolk flows warmly over my palate and down my throat. And indigestion is never a problem. Naturally, I use the finest ingredients: the freshest vegetables, fish straight from the water, the most delicately marbled meat. Everything must be done right. Just to make sure, a friend sent me the recipe for authentic homemade sausage, *andouillette de Troyes*, with three different kinds of meat braided in strips. Also, I scrupulously observe the rhythm of the seasons. Just now I am cooling my taste buds with melon and red fruit. I leave oysters and game for the autumn— should I feel like eating them, for I am becoming careful, even ascetic, in matters of diet. At the outset of my protracted fast, deprivation sent me constantly to my imaginary larder. I was gluttonous. But today I could almost be content with a good old proletarian hard sausage trussed in netting and suspended permanently from the ceiling in some corner of my head. A knobby Lyons rosette, for example, very dry and coarsely chopped. Every slice melts a little on your tongue before you start chewing to extract all its flavor. The origin of my addiction to sausage goes back forty years. Although still at an age for candy, I already preferred delicatessen meats, and my maternal grandfather's nurse noticed that whenever I visited the gloomy apartment on the Boulevard Raspail, I would ask her in a beguiling lisp for sausage. Skilled at indulging the desires of children and the elderly, she eventually pulled off a double coup, giving me a sausage and marrying my grandfather just before he died. My joy at receiving such a gift was in direct proportion to the annoyance the unexpected nuptials caused my family. I have only the vaguest picture of my grandfather: supine and stern-faced in the gloom, resembling Victor Hugo's portrait on the old five-hundred-franc notes in use at the time. I have a much clearer memory of that sausage lying incongruously among my Dinky Toys and picture books.

Guardian Angel

The identity badge pinned to Sandrine's white tunic says "Speech Therapist," but it should read "Guardian Angel." She is the one who set up the communication code without which I would be cut off from the world. But alas! while most of my friends have adopted the system, here at the hospital only Sandrine and a female psychologist use it. So I usually have the skimpiest arsenal of facial expressions, winks, and nods to ask people to shut the door, loosen a faucet, lower the volume on the TV, or fluff up a pillow. I do not succeed every time. As the weeks go by, this forced solitude has allowed me to acquire a certain stoicism and to realize that the hospital staff are of two kinds: the majority, who would not dream of leaving the room without first attempting to decipher my SOS messages; and the less conscientious minority, who make their getaway pretending not to notice my distress signals. Like that heartless oaf who switched off the Bordeaux-Munich soccer game at halftime, saying "Good night!" with a finality that left no hope of appeal. Quite apart from the practical drawbacks, this inability to communicate is somewhat wearing. Which explains the gratification I feel twice daily when Sandrine knocks, pokes her small chipmunk face through the door, and at once sends all gloomy thoughts packing. The invisible and eternally imprisoning diving bell seems less oppressive.

Speech therapy is an art that deserves to be more widely known. You cannot imagine the acrobatics your tongue mechanically performs in order to produce all the sounds of a language. Just now I am struggling with the letter *l,* a pitiful admission for an editor in chief who cannot even pronounce the name of his own magazine! On good days, between coughing fits, I muster enough energy and wind to be able to puff out one or two phonemes. On my birthday, Sandrine managed to get me to pronounce the whole alphabet more or less intelligibly. I could not have had a better present. It was as if those twenty-six letters had been wrenched from the void; my own hoarse voice seemed to emanate from a far-off country. The exhausting exercise left me feeling like a caveman discovering language for the first time. Sometimes the phone interrupts our work, and I take advantage of Sandrine's presence to be in touch with loved ones, to intercept and catch passing fragments of life, the way you catch a butterfly. My daughter, Céleste, tells me of her adventures with her pony. In five months she will be nine. My father tells me how hard it is to stay on his feet. He is fighting undaunted through his ninety-third year. These two are the outer links of the chain of love that surrounds and protects me. I often wonder about the effect of these one-way conversations on those at the other end of the line. I am overwhelmed by them. How dearly I would love to be able to respond with something other than silence to these tender calls. I know that some of them find it unbearable. Sweet Florence refuses to speak to me unless I first breathe noisily into the receiver that Sandrine holds glued to my ear. "Are you there, Jean-Do?" she asks anxiously over the air.

And I have to admit that at times I do not know anymore.

The Photo

The last time I saw my father, I shaved him. It was the week of my stroke. He was unwell, so I had spent the night at his small apartment near the Tuileries gardens in Paris. In the morning, after bringing him a cup of milky tea, I decided to rid him of his few days' growth of beard. The scene has remained engraved in my memory.

Hunched in the red-upholstered armchair where he sifts through the day's newspapers, my dad bravely endures the rasp of the razor attacking his loose skin. I wrap a big towel around his shriveled neck, daub thick lather over his face, and do my best not to irritate his skin, dotted here and there with small dilated capillaries. From age and fatigue, his eyes have sunk deep into their sockets, and his nose looks too prominent for his emaciated features. But, still flaunting the plume of hair— now snow white—that has always crowned his tall frame, he has lost none of his splendor.

All around us, a lifetime's clutter has accumulated; his room calls to mind one of those old persons' attics whose secrets only they can know—a confusion of old magazines, records

41

no longer played, miscellaneous objects. Photos from all the ages of man have been stuck into the frame of a large mirror. There is Dad, wearing a sailor suit and playing with a hoop before the Great War; my eight-year-old daughter in riding gear; and a black-and-white photo of myself on a miniature-golf course. I was eleven, my ears protruded, and I looked like a somewhat simpleminded schoolboy. Mortifying to realize that at that age I was already a confirmed dunce.

I complete my barber's duties by splashing my father with his favorite aftershave lotion. Then we say goodbye; this time, for once, he neglects to mention the letter in his writing desk where his last wishes are set out. We have not seen each other since. I cannot quit my seaside confinement. And he can no longer descend the magnificent staircase of his apartment building on his ninety-two-year-old legs. We are both locked-in cases, each in his own way: myself in my carcass, my father in his fourth-floor apartment. Now I am the one they shave every morning, and I often think of him while a nurse's aide laboriously scrapes my cheeks with a week-old blade. I hope that I was a more attentive Figaro.

Every now and then he calls, and I listen to his affectionate voice, which quivers a little in the receiver they hold to my ear. It cannot be easy for him to speak to a son who, as he well knows, will never reply. He also sent me the photo of me at the miniature-golf course. At first I did not understand why. It would have remained a mystery had someone not thought to look at the back of the print. Suddenly, in my own personal movie theater, the forgotten footage of a spring weekend began to unroll, when my parents and I had gone to take the air in a windy and not very sparkling seaside town. In his strong, angular handwriting, Dad had simply noted: *Berck-sur-Mer, April 1963.*

Yet Another
Coincidence

If you asked readers which of Alexandre
Dumas's literary heroes they would like to be,
they would pick D'Artagnan or Edmond
Dantès. No one would dream of choosing
Noirtier de Villefort, a somewhat sinister
character in *The Count of Monte Cristo*.
Described by Dumas as a living mummy, a man
three-quarters of the way into the grave, this
profoundly handicapped creature summons
up not dreams but shudders. The mute and
powerless possessor of the most terrible
secrets, he spends his life slumped in a wheelchair, able to communicate only by blinking
his eye: one blink means yes; two means no.
In fact, dear Grandpapa Noirtier, as his grand-
daughter affectionately calls him, is literature's
first—and so far only—case of locked-in syndrome.

As soon as my mind was clear of the thick
fog with which my stroke had shrouded it, I
began to think a lot about Grandpapa Noirtier.
I had just reread *The Count of Monte Cristo*, and
now here I was back in the heart of the book,

and in the worst of circumstances. Ironic—but that rereading had not been purely by chance. I had been toying with the idea of writing a modern, doubtless iconoclastic, version of the Dumas novel. Vengeance, of course, remained the driving force of the action, but the plot took place in our era, and Monte Cristo was a woman.

So I did not have time to commit this crime of lèse-majesté. As a punishment, I would have preferred to be transformed into M. Danglars, Franz d'Épinay, the Abbé Faria, or, at the very least, to copy out one thousand times: "I must not tamper with masterpieces." But the gods of literature and neurology decided otherwise.

Some evenings I have the impression that Grandpapa Noirtier patrols our corridors in a century-old wheelchair sadly in need of a drop of oil. To foil the decrees of fate, I am now planning a vast saga in which the key witness is not a paralytic but a runner. You never know. Perhaps it will work.

The Dream

As a rule, I do not recall my dreams. At the approach of day their plots inevitably fade. So why did last December's dreams etch themselves into my memory with the precision of a laser beam? Perhaps that is how it is with coma. Since you never return to reality, your dreams don't have the luxury of evaporating. Instead they pile up, one upon another, to form a long ongoing pageant whose episodes recur with the insistence of a soap opera. This evening, one such episode has come back to me.

In my dream, thick snow is falling. It lies a foot deep over the automobile graveyard my best friend and I are walking through, numb with cold. For three days, Bernard and I have been trying to get back to a France paralyzed by a general strike. We ended up in an Italian winter-sports resort, where we found a small local train heading for Nice. But at the French border a strikers' picket line interrupted our journey and bundled us out of the train and into this desolate landscape, without overcoats and wearing thin city shoes. A lofty overpass straddles the junkyard, as if vehicles falling from the bridge one hundred fifty feet above our heads have piled up here, one on top of another. Bernard and I have an appointment with an influential Italian businessman who has installed his headquarters in one massive pillar of the viaduct, far from prying eyes. We knock at a yellow steel door with the sign "Danger: High Voltage" and an instruction chart for treating electric shock. The door opens. The entrance is reminiscent of a garment-district outlet: jackets on a mobile rack, piles of trousers, boxes of shirts rising to the ceiling. I recognize the surly watchman who admits us by his shock of hair: Radovan Karadzic, leader of the Bosnian Serbs. "My friend is having trouble breathing," Bernard tells him. Laying down his machine gun, Karadzic performs a tracheotomy upon me on a hastily cleared table. Then we walk down ornate glass stairs to a study in the cellar. Its walls are lined with tan leather; deep armchairs and muted lighting give it the feel of a nightclub. Bernard confers with the owner, a clone of Fiat's elegant former chairman Gianni Agnelli, while a hostess with a Lebanese accent sits me down at a small bar. Instead of glasses and bottles, rows of plastic tubes dangle floorward like oxygen masks in an aircraft in distress. A barman motions me to put one in my mouth. I comply, and an amber ginger-flavored fluid begins to flow, flooding me with warmth from my toes to the roots of my hair. After a while

I want to stop drinking and get down off my stool. Yet I continue to swallow, unable to make the slightest move. I look frantically at the barman to attract his attention. He responds with an enigmatic smile. Around me, voices and faces become distorted. Bernard says something to me, but the sound emerging in slow motion from his mouth is incomprehensible. Instead I hear Ravel's *Bolero*. I have been completely drugged.

Eons later, I become aware of an alarm sounding. The hostess with the Lebanese accent hoists me on her back and climbs the staircase with me. "We have to get out: the police are on their way." Outside, night has fallen and the snow has stopped. An icy wind takes my breath away. The dazzling beam of a searchlight mounted on the overpass probes the forlorn automobile carcasses.

"Give up, you're surrounded!" blares a loudspeaker. We manage to get away, and I wander about, utterly lost. I long to escape, but every time the chance arises, a leaden torpor prevents me from taking even a single step. I am petrified, mummified, vitrified. If just one door stands between me and freedom, I am incapable of opening it. Yet that is not my only terror. For I am also the hostage of a mysterious cult, and I fear that my friends will fall into the same trap. I try desperately to warn them, but my dream conforms perfectly with reality. I am unable to utter a word.

Voice Offstage

I have known gentler awakenings. When I came to that late-January morning, the hospital ophthalmologist was leaning over me and sewing my right eyelid shut with a needle and thread, just as if he were darning a sock. Irrational terror swept over me. What if this man got carried away and sewed up my left eye as well, my only link to the outside world, the only window to my cell, the one tiny opening of my diving bell? Luckily, as it turned out, I wasn't plunged into darkness. He carefully packed away his sewing kit in padded tin boxes. Then, in the tones of a prosecutor demanding a maximum sentence for a repeat offender, he barked out: "Six months!" I fired off a series of questioning signals with my working eye, but this man—who spent his days peering into people's pupils—was apparently unable to interpret a simple look. With a big round head, a short body, and a fidgety manner, he was the very model of the couldn't-care-less doctor: arrogant, brusque, sarcastic—the kind who summons his patients for 8:00 a.m., arrives at 9:00, and departs at 9:05, after giving each of

51

them forty-five seconds of his precious time. Disinclined to chat with normal patients, he turned thoroughly evasive in dealing with ghosts of my ilk, apparently incapable of finding words to offer the slightest explanation. But I finally discovered why he had put a six-month seal on my eye: the lid was no longer fulfilling its function as a protective cover, and I ran the risk of an ulcerated cornea.

As the weeks went by, I wondered whether the hospital employed such an ungracious character deliberately—to serve as a focal point for the veiled mistrust the medical profession always arouses in long-term patients. A kind of scapegoat, in other words. If he leaves Berck, which seems likely, who will be left for me to sneer at? I shall no longer have the solitary, innocent pleasure of hearing his eternal question: "Do you see double?" and replying—deep inside—"Yes, I see two ass-holes, not one."

I need to feel strongly, to love and to admire, just as desperately as I need to breathe. A letter from a friend, a Balthus painting on a postcard, a page of Saint-Simon, give meaning to the passing hours. But to keep my mind sharp, to avoid descending into resigned indifference, I maintain a level of resentment and anger, neither too much nor too little, just as a pressure cooker has a safety valve to keep it from exploding.

And while we're on the subject, *The Pressure*

Cooker could be a title for the play I may write one day, based on my experiences here. I've also thought of calling it *The Eye* and, of course, *The Diving Bell.* You already know the plot and the setting. A hospital room in which Mr. L., a family man in the prime of life, is learning to live with locked-in syndrome brought on by a serious cerebrovascular accident. The play follows Mr. L.'s adventures in the medical world and his shifting relationships with his wife, his children, his friends, and his associates from the leading advertising agency he helped to found. Ambitious, somewhat cynical, heretofore a stranger to failure, Mr. L. takes his first steps into distress, sees all the certainties that buttressed him collapse, and discovers that his nearest and dearest are strangers. We could carry this slow transformation to the front seats of the balcony: a voice offstage would reproduce Mr. L.'s unspoken inner monologue as he faces each new situation. All that is left is to write the play. I have the final scene already: The stage is in darkness, except for a halo of light around the bed in center stage. Nighttime. Everyone is asleep. Suddenly Mr. L., inert since the curtain first rose, throws aside sheets and blankets, jumps from the bed, and walks around the eerily lit stage. Then it grows dark again, and you hear the voice offstage—Mr. L.'s inner voice—one last time:

"Damn! It was only a dream!"

My Lucky Day

This morning, with first light barely bathing Room 119, evil spirits descended on my world. For half an hour, the alarm on the machine that regulates my feeding tube has been beeping out into the void. I cannot imagine anything so inane or nerve-racking as this piercing *beep beep beep* pecking away at my brain. As a bonus, my sweat has unglued the tape that keeps my right eyelid closed, and the stuck-together lashes are tickling my pupil unbearably. And to crown it all, the end of my urinary catheter has become detached and I am drenched. Awaiting rescue, I hum an old song by Henri Salvador: "Don't you fret, baby, it'll be all right." And here comes the nurse. Automatically, she turns on the TV. A commercial, with a personal computer spelling out the question: "Were you born lucky?"

Our Very Own Madonna

When friends jokingly ask whether I have considered a pilgrimage to Lourdes, I tell them I've already made the trip. It was the end of the seventies. Joséphine and I were in a relationship that was a little too complicated to weather a traveling vacation together. It turned out to be one of those unstructured holidays that contain as many germs of potential discord as a day has minutes. We set out in the morning without knowing where we would sleep that night (and without knowing how we would reach our unknown destination). For two people to get along on such a trip requires a high degree of tactfulness. Joséphine was the kind of person who was prepared to do what it takes to get her own way. I tend to be like that too. For a whole week, her pale-blue convertible was the theater of an ongoing mobile domestic crisis. I had just finished a hiking trip in Ax-les-Thermes—an incongruous interval in a life devoted to everything except sport! The hike concluded at the Chambre d'Amour, a little beach on the Basque coast where Joséphine's uncle had a villa. From there, we made a tempestuous and magnificent crossing of the Pyrenees, leaving behind us a long trail of remarks on the order of "First of all, I never said any such thing!"

The prime bone of this quasi-marital contention was a fat book six or seven hundred pages long, with a black-and-white cover and an intriguing title. *Trail of the Snake* told the tale of Charles Sobraj, a kind of wayfaring guru who charmed and robbed Western travelers between Bombay and Kathmandu. The story of Sobraj, the half-French, half-Indian "snake" of the title, was true. Apart from that, I am quite unable to provide the slightest detail; it is even possible that my summary is inaccurate. But what I recall perfectly is the spell Charles Sobraj cast over me. On the way back from Andorra, I was still willing to lift my nose from the book to admire a landscape, but by the time we reached the Pic du Midi, in southern France, I refused point-blank to leave the car long enough for the stroll to the observation point. To be fair, a dense yellowish fog had rolled in over the mountain, reducing visibility and the attractions of such a stroll. Nevertheless, Joséphine dumped me there for a couple of hours while she sulked alone among the clouds. Was it to exorcise the serpent's spell that she insisted on a detour to Lourdes? Since I had never been to this world capital of miracles, I readily agreed. In any case, to my fevered brain, Charles Sobraj had blended into Bernadette, and the waters of the Adour River had mingled with those of the Ganges.

The next day, after having crossed a mountain pass on the Tour de France route whose incline struck me as exhausting even by car, we rolled into Lourdes. The heat was suffocating. Joséphine was driving; I sat beside her. And *Trail of the Snake,* swollen and dog-eared, was relegated to the backseat. I had not dared lay a finger on it since morning, Joséphine having decided that my passion for the exotic saga masked a lack of interest in her. It was the height of the pilgrimage season, and the city was jam-packed. Still, I undertook a systematic hunt for a hotel room, only to encounter—depending on the caliber of the hotel—dismissive shrugs or murmurs of "We're really sorry." Sweat had glued my shirt to my ribs, and the prospect of a fresh quarrel was looming by the time the receptionist at the Hôtel d'Angleterre—or d'Espagne, or des Balkans, or whatever—informed us of a cancellation, in the portentous tones of a lawyer announcing to a group of heirs the unexpected demise of a rich uncle. Yes, they had a vacancy. I refrained from saying "It's a miracle," for instinct told me that in Lourdes you did not joke about such things. The elevator, designed to accommodate stretchers, was vast, and in the shower ten minutes later, I realized that our bathroom was also equipped for the handicapped.

While Joséphine took her turn in the bathroom, I pounced, clad only in a towel, on that supreme oasis of the thirsty: the minibar. First I downed a half-bottle of mineral water at one swallow. Divine bottle, never will I forget the touch of your glass neck on my parched lips! Then I poured a glass of champagne for Joséphine and a gin and tonic for myself. Having thus performed my barman duties, I was furtively considering a strategic withdrawal to the adventures of Charles Sobraj. But instead of the hoped-for sedative effect, the champagne restored all Joséphine's tourist zeal. "I want to see the Madonna," she said, jumping up with her feet together, like François Mauriac in a famous photo.

So off we went, under a heavy, threatening sky, to see the holy site. We passed an unbroken column of wheelchairs led by volunteers who were clearly experienced at shepherding paraplegics. "Everyone into the basilica if it rains!" trumpeted the nun leading the procession, her headgear whipped by the wind, her rosary clasped firmly in her hand. I surreptitiously studied these invalids, their twisted hands, their closed faces, these small parcels of life hunched in upon themselves. One of them caught my eye, and I ventured a smile. He responded by sticking out his tongue, and I felt myself blush stupidly scarlet, as if caught out in some crime. Meanwhile, Joséphine, in pink sneakers, pink jeans, and pink sweatshirt, strode delightedly ahead through the midst of a somber mass (every French priest who still dressed like a priest seemed to have turned up for the occasion). Joséphine was nearly ecstatic when the chorus of robes took up the words "Appear to us, Madonna, we beg you on our knees," the chant of her childhood years. So fervent was the atmosphere that a casual observer might have thought himself outside Parc des Princes during a European Cup match.

A queue half a mile long, chanting Ave Marias, wound across the broad esplanade in front of the entrance to the grotto. I had never seen such a queue, except perhaps outside Lenin's tomb in Moscow.

"Listen, there's no way I'm going to wait in this!"

"Pity," Joséphine snapped. "It would do a sinner like you a lot of good!"

"Not at all. It could even be dangerous. What if someone in perfect health happened to be here when the Madonna appeared? One miracle, and he'd end up paralyzed."

A dozen heads turned to see who could have uttered these disrespectful words. "Idiot," muttered Joséphine. Then a rain shower diverted attention from me. At the very first drops, we witnessed the spontaneous generation of a forest of umbrellas, and the smell of hot dust floated in the air.

We were borne forward into the underground Basilica of St. Pius X, a gigantic prayer barn where Mass is celebrated from 6:00 a.m. to midnight, with a change of priest every two or three services. I had read in the guidebook that the concrete nave could accommodate several jumbo jets. I followed Joséphine to a bay with empty seats beneath one of the countless echoing loudspeakers that transmitted the ceremony. "Glory be to God in the highest... in the highest... in the highest..." At the elevation of the Host, the man next to me, a well-prepared pilgrim, pulled racegoer's binoculars from his backpack to watch the proceedings. Other believers had makeshift periscopes of the kind you see at parades. Joséphine's father had often told me how he started out in life selling these kinds of gadgets outside metro stations. This did not prevent him from becoming a giant of broadcasting. Now he made use of his barker's skills to describe royal weddings, earthquakes, and prizefights for his audience. Outside, it had stopped raining. The air was cooler. "Shopping," said Joséphine. Anticipating this eventuality, I had already marked out the main thoroughfare, in which souvenir shops jostled one another as intimately as in an Oriental bazaar, offering the most extravagant smorgasbord of devotional objects.

Joséphine was a collector: old perfume bottles, rustic canvases complete with cattle (singly or in herds), plates of make-believe food of the kind that substitute for menus in Tokyo restaurant windows. In short, during her frequent travels she bought everything unspeakably kitsch she could lay her hands on. In Lourdes, it was love at first sight. There she sat in the window of the fourth shop on the left, surrounded by a jumble of religious medals, Swiss cuckoo clocks, decorated cheese platters, and—apparently waiting just for Joséphine— an adorable stucco bust haloed with winking bulbs, like a Christmas tree decoration.

"There's my Madonna!" Joséphine exulted.

"It's my present," I said at once, with no inkling of the exorbitant sum the shopkeeper would soon extort from me (alleging that it was one of a kind). That evening, in our hotel room, we celebrated our acquisition, its flickering holy light bathing us and casting fantastic dancing shadows on the ceiling.

"Joséphine, I think we're going to have to split up when we get back to Paris."

"Do you think I don't realize that?"

"But Jo..."

She was asleep. She had the gift of falling into instant sheltering slumber when a situation annoyed her. She could take a vacation from life for five minutes or several hours. For a while I watched the wall behind our pillows jump into and out of darkness. What demon could have induced people to line a whole room with orange fabric?

Since Joséphine was still sleeping, I cautiously dressed and left to engage in one of my favorite pastimes: night walking. It was my personal way of battling misfortune: just walking until I dropped. Out on the street, Dutch youths guzzled beer from big mugs. They had torn holes in garbage bags to make raincoats. Stout bars blocked the way to the grotto, but at intervals I saw the glow of hundreds of guttering candles. Much later, my wanderings brought me back to the street with the souvenir stores. In the fourth window, an identical Mary had taken the place of ours. Then I turned back to the hotel; from very far away I saw the window of our room twinkling in the gloom. I climbed the stairs, careful not to disturb the night watchman's dreams. *Trail of the Snake* sat on my pillow like a jewel in its setting. "Well, well," I murmured. "Charles Sobraj! I'd forgotten all about him."

I recognized Joséphine's writing. A huge "I" was scrawled across page 168. It was the start of a message that took up two whole chapters of the book and left them totally unreadable.

"I love you, you idiot. Be kind to your poor Joséphine."

Luckily I had read these pages already.

When I switched off the Holy Virgin, day was just breaking.

Through a Glass, Darkly

Hunched in my wheelchair, I watch my children surreptitiously as their mother pushes me down the hospital corridor. While I have become something of a zombie father, Théophile and Céleste are very much flesh and blood, energetic and noisy. I will never tire of seeing them walk alongside me, just walking, their confident expressions masking the unease weighing on their small shoulders. As he walks, Théophile dabs with a Kleenex at the thread of saliva escaping my closed lips. His movements are tentative, at once tender and fearful, as if he were dealing with an animal of unpredictable reactions. As soon as we slow down, Céleste cradles my head in her bare arms, covers my forehead with noisy kisses, and says over and over, "You're my dad, you're my dad," as if in incantation.

Today is Father's Day. Until my stroke, we had felt no need to fit this made-up holiday into our emotional calendar. But today we spend the whole of the symbolic day together, affirming that even a rough sketch, a shadow, a tiny fragment of a dad is still a dad. I am torn between joy at seeing them living, moving, laughing, or crying for a few hours, and fear that the sight of all these sufferings—beginning with mine—is not the ideal entertainment for a boy of ten and his eight-year-old sister. However, we have made the wise collective decision not to sugarcoat anything.

We install ourselves at the Beach Club—my name for a patch of sand dune open to sun and wind, where the hospital has obligingly set out tables, chairs, and umbrellas, and even planted a few buttercups, which grow in the sand amid the weeds. In this neutral zone on the beach, a transition between hospital and everyday life, one could easily imagine some good fairy turning every wheelchair into a chariot. "Want to play hangman?" asks Théophile, and I ache to tell him that I have enough on my plate playing quadriplegic. But my communication system disqualifies repartee: the keenest rapier grows dull and falls flat when it takes several minutes to thrust it home. By the time you strike, even you no longer understand what had seemed so witty before you started to dictate it, letter by letter. So the rule is to avoid impulsive sallies. It deprives conversation of its sparkle, all those gems you bat back and forth like a ball—and I count this forced lack of humor one of the great drawbacks of my condition.

But we can certainly play hangman, the national preteen sport. I guess a letter, then another, then stumble on the third. My heart is not in the game. Grief surges over me. His face not two feet from mine, my son Théophile sits patiently waiting—and I, his father, have lost the simple right to ruffle his bristly hair, clasp his downy neck, hug his small, lithe, warm body tight against me. There are no words to express it. My condition is monstrous, iniquitous, revolting, horrible. Suddenly I can take no more. Tears well and my throat emits a hoarse rattle that startles Théophile. Don't be scared, little man. I love you. Still engrossed in the game, he moves in for the kill. Two more letters: he has won and I have lost. On a corner of the page he completes his drawing of the gallows, the rope, and the condemned man.

Meanwhile, Céleste is doing cartwheels on the sand. Perhaps some compensatory mechanism is at work, for ever since the act of blinking became the equivalent of weight lifting for me, she has turned into a genuine acrobat. With the flexibility of a cat, she does a back flip, a handstand, a somersault, and a whole series of daring leaps and twists. She has recently added tightrope walker to the long list of professions she envisions for her future (after schoolteacher, supermodel, and florist). With the onlookers at the Beach Club won over by her display, our budding entertainer now launches into a song-and-dance act, to the great dismay of Théophile, who more than anything else hates drawing attention to himself. As shy and reclusive as his sister is outgoing, he wholeheartedly hated me the day I sought and obtained permission to ring the school bell for the first day of class. No one can predict whether Théophile will be happy; but it is certain that he will live in the shadows.

I wonder how Céleste has managed to accumulate such a repertoire of sixties songs. Johnny Hallyday, Sylvie Vartan, Sheila, Clo-Clo François, Françoise Hardy—all the stars of that golden era. Alongside universally familiar numbers, Céleste sings forgotten hits that trail clouds of nostalgia in their wake. Not since I was twelve, when I endlessly played it on my record player, have I heard the Clo-Clo François 45-rpm "Poor Little Rich Girl." Yet as soon as Céleste begins it—somewhat off-key—every note, every verse, every detail of backup and orchestration, comes back to me with startling precision, right down to the sound of the sea that filters through the opening bars. Once again I see the album cover, the singer's photo, his striped button-down shirt. I longed for a shirt like his, but for me it was unattainable: my mother considered it tacky. I even relive the Saturday afternoon when I bought the record. My father's cousin kept a tiny record store in the lower level of the Gare du Nord. He was a good-natured giant with a yellow Gitane cigarette dangling eternally from the corner of his mouth. "Poor little rich girl, alone on the beach, alone and so rich..." Time marches on, and people have since disappeared. Mama died first. Next, Clo-Clo François was electrocuted. Then my father's gentle cousin, whose business had gone downhill, gave up the ghost, leaving an inconsolable tribe of children and animals behind. My closet is now full of button-down shirts, and I believe the small record store now sells chocolates. Since the Berck train leaves from the Gare du Nord, perhaps one day I shall ask someone to check on the way through.

"Well done, Céleste!" cries Sylvie. "Maman, I'm bored," Théophile at once complains. It is 5:00 p.m. The hospital chimes, which usually strike me as cheerful, assume funereal tones as the time for farewells draws near. Wind begins to whip up the sand. The tide has gone out so far that swimmers look like tiny dots on the horizon. The children run to stretch their legs on the beach once more before leaving, and Sylvie and I remain alone and silent, her hand squeezing my inert fingers. Behind dark glasses that reflect a flawless sky, she softly weeps over our shattered lives.

We return to my room for the final leave-taking. "How do you feel, Pop?" asks Théophile. His pop's throat is tight, his hands are sunburned, and his bottom hurts from sitting on it too long, but he has had a wonderful day. And what about you kids, what will you carry back from this field trip into my endless solitude?

They have left. The car will already be

speeding toward Paris. I sink into contemplation of a drawing brought by Céleste, which we immediately pinned to the wall: a kind of two-headed fish with blue-lashed eyes and multicolored scales. But what is interesting in the drawing is its overall shape, which bears a disconcerting resemblance to the mathematical symbol for infinity. Sun streams in through the window. It is the hour when its rays fall straight upon my pillow. In the commotion of departure, I forgot to signal for the curtains to be drawn. A nurse will be in before the world comes to an end.

Paris

I am fading away. Slowly but surely. Like the sailor who watches the home shore gradually disappear, I watch my past recede. My old life still burns within me, but more and more of it is reduced to the ashes of memory.

Yet since taking up residence in my diving bell, I have made two brief trips to the world of Paris medicine to hear the verdict pronounced on me from the diagnostic heights. On the first occasion, my emotions got the better of me when my ambulance happened to pass the ultramodern high-rise where I once followed the reprehensible calling of editor in chief of a famous women's magazine. First I recognized the building next door—a sixties antiquity, now scheduled to be demolished, according to the billboard out front. Then I saw our own glass facade, airily reflecting clouds and airplanes. On the sidewalk were a few of those familiar-looking faces that one passes every day for ten years without ever being able to put a name to them. When I thought I glimpsed someone I actually knew, walking behind a woman with her hair in a bun and a burly man in work clothes, I nearly unscrewed my head to see.

Perhaps someone had caught sight of my ambulance from our sixth-floor offices. I shed a few tears as we passed the corner café where I used to drop in for a bite. I can weep quite discreetly. People think my eye is watering.

The second time I went to Paris, four months later, I was unmoved by it. The streets were decked out in summer finery, but for me it was still winter, and what I saw through the ambulance windows was just a movie background. Filmmakers call the process a "rear-screen projection," with the hero's car speeding along a road that unrolls behind him on a studio wall. Hitchcock films owe much of their poetry to the use of this process in its early, unperfected stages. My own crossing of Paris left me indifferent. Yet nothing was missing—housewives in flowered dresses and youths on roller skates, revving buses, messengers cursing on their scooters. The Place de l'Opéra, straight out of a Dufy canvas. The treetops foaming like surf against glass building fronts, wisps of cloud in the sky. Nothing was missing, except me. I was elsewhere.

The Vegetable

"On June 8 it will be six months since my new life began. Your letters are accumulating on the dresser, your drawings on my wall, and since I cannot hope to answer each one of you, I have decided to issue these samizdat bulletins to report on my life, my progress, and my hopes. At first I refused to believe that anything serious had happened. In my semiconscious state following the coma, I thought I would shortly be back in my Paris stamping grounds, with just a couple of canes to help me along."

Those were the first words of the first mailing of my monthly letter from Berck, which I decided in late spring to send to my friends and associates. Addressed to some sixty people, that first bulletin caused a mild stir and repaired some of the damage caused by rumor. The city, that monster with a hundred mouths and a thousand ears, a monster that knows nothing but says everything, had written me off. At the Café de Flore, one of those base camps of Parisian snobbery that send up rumors like flights of carrier pigeons, some close friends of mine overheard a conversation at the next table.

The gossipers were as greedy as vultures who have just discovered a disemboweled antelope. "Did you know that Bauby is now a total vegetable?" said one. "Yes, I heard. A complete vegetable," came the reply. The word "vegetable" must have tasted sweet on the know-it-all's tongue, for it came up several times between mouthfuls of Welsh rarebit. The tone of voice left no doubt that henceforth I belonged on a vegetable stall and not to the human race. France was at peace; one couldn't shoot the bearers of bad news. Instead I would have to rely on myself if I wanted to prove that my IQ was still higher than a turnip's.

Thus was born a collective correspondence that keeps me in touch with those I love. And my hubris has had gratifying results. Apart from an irrecoverable few who maintain a stubborn silence, everybody now understands that he can join me in my diving bell, even if sometimes the diving bell takes me into unexplored territory.

I receive remarkable letters. They are opened for me, unfolded, and spread out before my eyes in a daily ritual that gives the arrival of the mail the character of a hushed and holy ceremony. I carefully read each letter myself. Some of them are serious in tone, discussing the meaning of life, invoking the supremacy of the soul, the mystery of every existence. And by a curious reversal, the people who focus most closely on these fundamental questions tend to be people

I had known only superficially. Their small talk had masked hidden depths. Had I been blind and deaf, or does it take the harsh light of disaster to show a person's true nature?

Other letters simply relate the small events that punctuate the passage of time: roses picked at dusk, the laziness of a rainy Sunday, a child crying himself to sleep. Capturing the moment, these small slices of life, these small gusts of happiness, move me more deeply than all the rest. A couple of lines or eight pages, a Middle Eastern stamp or a suburban postmark... I hoard all these letters like treasure. One day I hope to fasten them end to end in a half-mile streamer, to float in the wind like a banner raised to the glory of friendship.

It will keep the vultures at bay.

Outing

Stifling heat. But I would like to get out. It has been weeks, perhaps months, since I last left the hospital grounds for my wheelchair ride on the promenade along the shore. Last time it was still winter. Icy gusts whipped up clouds of sand, and the few thickly muffled strollers leaned purposefully into the wind. Today I would like to see Berck in summer attire, to see the beach—which was deserted all winter—packed with carefree July crowds. To reach the street from Sorrel, one has to cross three parking lots, whose rough, uneven surface sorely tries the buttocks. I had forgotten how grueling this route was, with its puddles and its potholes, its cars inconsiderately parked on the sidewalks.

And then at last the sea. Beach umbrellas, sailboats, and a human rampart of swimmers complete the postcard effect. A vacation sea, gentle and unthreatening. Nothing like the steel reflection visible from the hospital terraces. And yet these are the same troughs, the same swells, the same misty horizon.

We thread our way through a moving forest of ice-cream cones and crimson thighs. Easy

77

to imagine licking a drop of vanilla from young, sun-reddened skin... No one pays me any real attention. Wheelchairs are as commonplace at Berck as Ferraris at Monte Carlo, and poor dislocated wheezing devils like me are everywhere. This afternoon, Claude (the young woman to whom I am dictating this book) and Brice are with me. I have known Claude for two weeks, Brice for twenty-five years. It is strange to hear my old partner in crime telling Claude about me. My quick temper, my love of books, my immoderate taste for good food, my red convertible—nothing is left out. Like a storyteller exhuming the legends of a lost civilization. "I didn't realize you were like that," says Claude. My present life is divided between those who knew me before and all the others. What kind of person will those who know me now think I was? I do not even have a photo to show them.

We stop at the top of a big stairway that goes down to the beach bar and to a long line of pastel-colored cabanas. The stairs remind me of the entrance to the Porte d'Auteuil metro station in Paris. I used to climb them as a child when returning from the old Molitor swimming pool, my eyes red with chlorine. The pool was demolished a few years ago. As for stairs, they are now just dead ends for me.

"Want to turn back?" asks Brice. I protest, shaking my head vigorously. No question of turning around until we have reached our real goal. We move quickly past an old-fashioned wooden carousel, whose shrieking calliope pierces my eardrums. We pass a well-known hospital character we call "Fangio." Tall, dark-haired, athletic-looking, Fangio is rigid as a poker. Unable to sit, he is permanently condemned to either a vertical or a horizontal position. He gets about at amazing speed, lying flat on his stomach on a vehicle he operates himself, parting the crowds with yells of "Look out—here comes Fangio!" I know who he is, but who is he really? I have no idea. Finally we reach the farthest point of our journey, the very end of the promenade. I have not insisted on coming all this way just to gaze at the flawless seascape. I have come to gorge on the aromas emanating from a modest shack by the path leading away from the beach. Claude and Brice bring me to a halt downwind. My nostrils quiver with pleasure as they inhale a robust odor—intoxicating to me but one that most mortals cannot abide. "Ooh!" says a disgusted voice behind me. "What a stench!"

But I never tire of the smell of french fries.

Twenty to One

That's it—it's come back to me. The horse's name was Mithra-Grandchamp.

Vincent must be on his way through Abbeville by now. If you are driving from Paris, this is the point where the trip begins to seem long. You have left the unencumbered thruway for a two-lane road choked by endless lines of cars and trucks.

When this story takes place, more than ten years ago, Vincent, myself, and a few others had had the extraordinary good fortune to be putting out a daily newspaper, which has since disappeared. The owner, a press-infatuated industrialist, was brave enough to entrust his baby to the youngest editorial team in Paris, at the very moment when dark political and financial forces were plotting to snatch its controls. Without knowing it, we were the last cards he was to lay on the table, and we hurled ourselves one thousand percent into the fray.

By now Vincent has reached the intersection where he leaves the Rouen and Crotoy roads on his left and takes the minor road leading through a string of small townships to

Berck. Drivers who don't know the way are led astray by its twists and turns. But Vincent, who has come to see me several times, keeps his bearings. To his sense of direction he adds—carried to the extreme—a sense of loyalty.

We worked seven days a week. Arriving early, leaving late. We worked on weekends and sometimes all night, blissfully doing the work of a dozen with five pairs of hands. Vincent had ten major ideas every week: three brilliant, five good, and two ridiculous. It was part of my job to force him to choose among them, which went against his impatient grain. He would have preferred to act at once on every one of them, good and bad.

I can hear him now, fuming at the steering wheel and cursing the Highway Department. In two years the thruway will reach Berck, but right now it is just an endless construction site, pushing forward slowly from behind a screen of bulldozers and heavy-duty vehicles.

We were inseparable. We lived, ate, drank, slept, and dreamed only of and for the paper. Whose idea was that afternoon at the racetrack? It was a fine winter Sunday, blue, cold, and dry, and the horses were running at Vincennes. Neither of us was a racing fan, but the track correspondent valued us highly enough to treat us to lunch at the Vincennes restaurant and to give us the password to the Aladdin's cave of racing: a tip. Mithra-Grandchamp was a sure thing, he told us, a guaranteed winner, and since the odds on him were twenty to one, a fat little profit—much better than municipal bonds—seemed likely.

Now Vincent is on the outskirts of Berck and—like all my visitors—is wondering what the hell he is doing here.

We had eaten an enjoyable lunch that day in the restaurant overlooking the racetrack. The large dining room was frequented by gangsters in their Sunday suits, pimps, parolees, and other shady characters who gravitate naturally to horse racing. Sated, we puffed greedily on long cigars and awaited the fourth race. In that hothouse atmosphere, criminal records bloomed like orchids all around us.

Reaching the seafront, Vincent turns and drives along the promenade. The throng of summer visitors eclipses his winter memories of a frigid, deserted Berck.

At Vincennes, we lingered so long in the dining room that the race came and went without us. The betting counter slammed shut under our noses before I had time to pull out the roll of banknotes the people back at the paper had entrusted to me. Despite our attempts at discretion, Mithra-Grandchamp's name had made the rounds of the newspaper. Rumor had turned him into a mythic beast, and everyone was determined to bet on him. All we could do was watch the race and hope... At the last turn, Mithra-Grandchamp began to pull away. Entering the final stretch, he had a lead of five lengths, and we watched in a dream as he crossed the finish line a good forty yards ahead of his closest pursuer. Back at the paper, they must have been going wild around the TV screen.

Vincent's car slips into the hospital parking lot. Brilliant sunshine. This is where my visitors, hearts in mouths, need fortitude to brave the few yards that separate me from the world: the automatic glass doors, elevator number 7, and the horrible little corridor leading to Room 119. All you can see through the half-open doors are bedridden wretches whom fate has cast to the far edge of life. Some visitors probably stand for a moment outside my room so that they can greet me with firmer voices and drier eyes. When they finally come in, they are gasping for air like divers whose oxygen has failed them. I even know of some who turned tail and fled back to Paris, their resolve abandoning them on my very threshold.

Vincent knocks and enters soundlessly. I have become so inured to the look on people's faces that I scarcely notice the transient gleam of fear. Or in any case, it no longer shakes me quite so much. I try to compose features atrophied by paralysis into what I hope is a welcoming smile. Vincent answers this grimace with a kiss on my forehead. He hasn't changed. His crest of red hair, his sullen expression, his stocky physique, his habit of shifting from one foot to the other, give him the look of a Welsh shop steward visiting a mate injured in a mine explosion. Vincent bobs forward like a prizefighter in the tough lightweight division. On Mithra-Grandchamp day, after that disastrous win, he had simply muttered: "Idiots! We're complete idiots! When we get back to the office we'll be history!" His favorite expression.

Frankly, I had forgotten Mithra-Grandchamp. The memory of that event has only just come back to me, now doubly painful: regret for a vanished past and, above all, remorse for lost opportunities. Mithra-Grandchamp is the women we were unable to love, the chances we failed to seize, the moments of happiness we allowed to drift away. Today it seems to me that my whole life was nothing but a string of those small near misses: a race whose result we know beforehand but in which we fail to bet on the winner. By the way, we managed to pay back all our colleagues.

The Duck Hunt

On top of the various discomforts that accompany locked-in syndrome, I suffer from a serious hearing disorder. My right ear is completely blocked, and my left ear amplifies and distorts all sounds farther than ten feet away. When a plane tows an ad for the local theme park over the beach, I could swear that a coffee mill has been grafted onto my eardrum. But that noise is only fleeting. Much more disturbing is the continuous racket that assails me from the corridor whenever they forget to shut my door despite all my efforts to alert people to my hearing problems. Heels clatter on the linoleum, carts crash into one another, hospital workers call to one another with the voices of stockbrokers trying to liquidate their holdings, radios nobody listens to are turned on, and on top of everything else, a floor waxer sends out an auditory foretaste of hell. There are also a few frightful patients. I know some whose only pleasure is to listen to the same cassette over and over. I had a very young neighbor who was given a velveteen duck equipped with a sophisticated detection device. It emitted a reedy, piercing quack whenever anyone entered the room—in other words, twenty-five times a day. Luckily the little patient went home before I could carry out my plan to exterminate the duck. I am keeping my scheme in readiness, though: you never know what horrors tearful families may bestow on their young. But the first prize for eccentric neighbors goes to a woman who emerged demented from a coma. She bit nurses, seized male orderlies by their genitals, and was unable to request a glass of water without screaming "Fire!" At first these false alarms had everyone dashing into action; then, weary of the struggle, they let her screaming fill all hours of the day and night. Her antics gave our neurology section a heady "cuckoo's nest" atmosphere, and I was almost sorry when they took our friend away to yell "Help! Murder!" elsewhere.

Far from such din, when blessed silence returns, I can listen to the butterflies that flutter inside my head. To hear them, one must be calm and pay close attention, for their wingbeats are barely audible. Loud breathing is enough to drown them out. This is astonishing: my hearing does not improve, yet I hear them better and better. I must have butterfly hearing.

Sunday

Through the window I watch the reddish-yellow hospital buildings light up under the sun's first rays. The brickwork takes on exactly the same shade of pink as the Greek grammar book I had in high school. I wasn't a brilliant Hellenist (to put it mildly), but I love that warm, deep shade: it still conjures up for me a world of books and study, in which we consorted with Alcibiades' dog and the heroes of Thermopylae. "Antique pink" is what hardware stores call it. It has absolutely no resemblance to the cotton-candy pink of the hospital corridors. And even less to the mauve that coats the baseboards and window frames in my room, making them look like the wrapping on a cheap perfume.

Sunday. I dread Sunday, for if I am unlucky enough to have no visitors, there will be nothing at all to break the dreary passage of the hours. No physical therapist, no speech pathologist, no shrink. Sunday is a long stretch of desert, its only oasis a sponge bath even more perfunctory than usual. On Sundays the nursing staff is plunged into gloomy lethargy by the delayed effects of Saturday-night drinking, coupled with regret at missing the family picnic, the trip to the fair, or the shrimp fishing on account of the Sunday duty roster. The bath I am given bears more resemblance to drawing and quartering than to hydrotherapy. A triple dose of the finest eau de toilette fails to mask the reality: I stink.

Sunday. If the TV is turned on, it is vital to have made the right decision. It is almost a matter of strategy. For three or four hours are likely to go by before the return of the kindly soul who can change channels. Sometimes it is wiser to forgo an interesting program if it is followed by a tearful soap opera, a silly game show, or a raucous talk show. Violent applause hurts my ears. I prefer the peace of documentaries on art, history, or animals. I watch them without the sound, the way you watch flames in a fireplace.

Sunday. The bell gravely tolls the hours. The small Health Department calendar on the wall, whittled away day by day, announces that it is already August. Mysterious paradox: time, motionless here, gallops out there. In my contracted world, the hours drag on but the months flash by. I can't believe it's August. Friends, their wives and children, have scattered to the summer winds. In my thoughts I steal into their summer quarters—never mind if doing so tugs at my heart. In Brittany, a pack of children returns from the market on bikes, every face radiant with laughter. Some of these kids have long since entered the age of major adolescent concerns, but along these rhododendron-lined Breton roads, everyone rediscovers lost innocence. This afternoon, they will be boating around the island, the small outboards laboring against the current. Someone will be stretched out in the bow, eyes closed, arm trailing in the cool water. In the south of France, a burning sun drives you to seek the cool depths of the house. You fill sketchbooks with watercolors. A small cat with a broken leg seeks shady corners in the priest's garden, and a little farther on, in the flat Camargue delta country, a cluster of young bulls skirts a marsh that gives off a smell of aniseed. And all over the country, activities are under way for the great domestic event of the day. I know mothers everywhere are tired of preparing it, but for me it is a legendary forgotten ritual: lunch.

Sunday. I contemplate my books, piled up on the windowsill to constitute a small library: a rather useless one, for today no one will come to read them for me. Seneca, Zola, Chateaubriand, and Valéry Larbaud are right there, three feet away, just out of reach. A very black fly settles on my nose. I waggle my head to unseat him. He digs in. Olympic wrestling is child's play compared to this. Sunday.

The Ladies
of Hong Kong

I loved to travel. Fortunately I have stored away
enough pictures, smells, and sensations over
the course of the years to enable me to leave
Berck far behind on days when a leaden sky
rules out any chance of going outdoors. They
are strange wanderings: The sour smell of a
New York bar. The odor of poverty in a
Rangoon market. Little bits of the world.
The white icy nights of Saint Petersburg or the
unbelievably molten sun at Furnace Creek in
the Nevada desert. This week has been somewhat special. At dawn every day I have flown
to Hong Kong, where there is a conference for
the international editions of my magazine.
Note that I still say "my magazine," despite
the misleading nature of the words, as if that
possessive pronoun were one of the fragile
threads linking me to the living world.

In Hong Kong, I have a little trouble finding my way, for unlike many of my other des-
tinations, this city is one I have never actually
visited. Every time the opportunity arose, a
malicious fate kept me from my goal. When

I did not fall sick on the eve of a departure, I lost my passport, or a reporting assignment sent me elsewhere. In short, chance always turned me back at the border. Once, I gave up my seat for Jean-Paul K., who at that time had not yet been taken hostage by the Hezbollah. He would spend several years in a darkened Beirut dungeon, endlessly reciting the wines of the Bordeaux Classification of 1855 to keep from going mad. On his return from Hong Kong, he brought me a cordless phone, at that time the very latest thing. I remember his laughing eyes behind their round glasses. I was very fond of Jean-Paul, but I never saw him again after his release from Beirut. I suppose I was ashamed of playing at being editor in chief in the frothy world of fashion magazines while he wrestled with life on its most brutal terms. Now I am the prisoner and he the free man. And since I don't have the châteaux of the Médoc region at my fingertips, I have had to choose another kind of litany to fill my empty hours: I count the countries where my magazine is published. There are already twenty-eight members in this United Nations of international glamour.

And where are they now, all my beautiful colleagues who worked so tirelessly as ambassadors of French style? They would stand in the conference rooms of international hotels, fielding a daylong barrage of questions in Chinese, English, Thai, Portuguese, or Czech, as they tried to answer that most metaphysical of questions: "Who is the typical *Elle* woman?" I picture them now wandering about Hong Kong, walking down neon-bright streets where pocket computers and noodle soup are sold, trotting behind the eternal bow tie of our chief executive officer as he leads his troops to the charge. Part Cyrano, part Bonaparte, he slows his pace only before the highest skyscrapers, and then only to scowl at them as though about to devour them.

Which way, General? Should we take the hydrofoil and gamble away a handful of dollars in Macao, or should we repair to the Felix Bar in the Peninsula Hotel, decorated by the French designer Philippe S.? Vanity impels me toward the second option. The fact is, my likeness adorns the back of a chair in that lofty luxurious watering hole. I, who hate to have my photo taken, was one of dozens of Parisians whose portraits Philippe S. incorporated into the decor. That photo, of course, was taken some weeks before fate turned me into a scarecrow. I have no idea whether my chair is more or less popular than the others, but if you go there, for God's sake don't tell the barman what happened to me. They say that all Chinese are superstitious, and if my true fate were known, not one of those charming little Chinese miniskirts would ever dare sit on me again.

The Message

Although my own corner of the hospital has the look of an expensive private school, one would never mistake the cafeteria crowd for members of the Dead Poets Society. The girls have hard eyes, the boys tattoos and sometimes rings on their fingers. There they sit, chain-smoking and talking about fist-fights and motorbikes. Their already stooped shoulders seem to bear a heavy cross. Cruel fate has cursed them, and their stay at Berck is just one more stage between an abused childhood and a jobless future. When I am wheeled through their smoke-filled lair, the silence becomes deafening; I see neither pity nor compassion in their eyes.

Through the open cafeteria window you can hear the beating of the hospital's bronze heart: the bell that makes the firmament vibrate four times an hour. On a table cluttered with empty cups stands a small typewriter with a sheet of pink paper stuck in the roller. Although at the moment the page is utterly blank, I am convinced that someday there will be a message for me there. I am waiting.

At the Wax Museum

In a dream last night, I visited Paris's wax museum, the Musée Grévin. It had changed. There was the same entrance, in turn-of-the-century style, the same distorting mirrors, the same chamber of horrors, but the galleries displaying contemporary figures were gone. In the first rooms, the characters on exhibit were in street clothes, and I did not recognize them until I mentally put them in white hospital uniforms. Then I realized that these boys in T-shirts and girls in miniskirts, this housewife frozen with teapot in hand, this crash-helmeted youth, were all in fact the nurses and orderlies of both sexes who took turns appearing morning and night at my hospital bedside. They were all there, fixed in wax: gentle, rough, caring, indifferent, hardworking, lazy, the ones you can make contact with and those to whom you are just another patient.

At first some of the staff had terrified me. I saw them only as my jailers, as accomplices in some awful plot. Later I hated some of them, those who wrenched my arm while putting me in my wheelchair, or left me all night

99

long with the TV on, or let me lie in a painful position despite my protests. For a few minutes or a few hours I would cheerfully have killed them. Later still, as time cooled my fiercest rages, I got to know them better. They carried out as best they could their delicate mission: to ease our burden a little when our crosses bruised our shoulders too painfully.

I gave them nicknames known only to me, so that when they entered my room I could hail them in my thunderous inner voice: "Hey, Blue Eyes! Morning, Big Bird!" They of course remained unaware. The one who dances around my bed and strikes an Elvis pose as he asks "How are you doing?" is "David Bowie." "Prof" makes me laugh, with his baby face and gray hair and the gravity with which he utters the unvarying judgment: "So far, so good." "Rambo" and "Terminator," as you might imagine, are not exactly models of gentleness. I prefer "Thermometer"; her dedication would be beyond reproach if she did not regularly forget the implement she thrusts under my armpit.

In my dream, the museum sculptor was not altogether successful in capturing the smiles and scowls of Berck's hospital personnel, northerners whose ancestors have always lived on this strip of France between the Channel coast and the rich fields of Picardy. They readily lapse into their local patois as soon as they are alone together. To get them right you would need the talent of one of those medieval miniaturists whose magic brush brought to life the folk who once thronged the roads of Flanders. Our artist does not possess such skill. Yet he has managed to capture the youthful charm of the student nurses with their dimpled country-girl arms and full pink cheeks. As I left the room, I realized that I was fond of all these torturers of mine.

Entering the next exhibit, I was surprised to find myself back in Room 119, apparently reproduced down to the last detail. But as I got closer, the photos, drawings, and posters on my walls turned out to be a patchwork of ill-defined colors. Like an Impressionist painting, it was a pattern intended to create an illusion at a certain distance. There was no one on the bed, just a hollow in the middle of the yellow sheets bathed in pallid light. And here I had no problem identifying the watchers on either side of the bed: they were members of the personal bodyguard that spontaneously sprang up around me immediately after the disaster.

Michel, seated on a stool and conscientiously scribbling in the notebook where visitors set down all my remarks. Anne-Marie, arranging a bouquet of forty roses. Bernard, holding a memoir of diplomatic life in one hand and with the other executing a theatrical barrister's gesture that was pure Daumier. Perched on the end of his nose, his steel-rimmed glasses completed the picture of a distinguished courtroom orator. Florence, pinning children's drawings on a corkboard, her black hair framing a sad smile. And Patrick, leaning against a wall, apparently lost in thought. Looking almost ready to leap into life, the group projected great tenderness, a shared sorrow, an accumulation of the affectionate gravity I feel whenever these friends come to see me.

I tried to continue the tour and see what fresh surprises the museum had in store, but in a gloomy corridor a guard turned his flashlight full on my face. I had to shut my eyes tight. When I awoke, a real nurse with plump arms was leaning over me, her penlight in her hand: "Your sleeping pill. Do you want it now, or shall I come back in an hour?"

The Mythmaker

On the benches of the Paris school where I wore
out my first pair of jeans, I made friends with
a skinny, red-faced boy named Olivier, whose
runaway mythomania made his company irre-
sistible. With him around, there was no need
to go to the movies. Olivier's friends had the
best seats in the house, and the film was a miracle of invention. On Monday he would amaze
us with a weekend saga straight out of *A
Thousand and One Nights.* If he had not spent
Sunday with Johnny Hallyday, it was because
he had gone to London to see the new James
Bond, unless he had been driving the latest
Honda. (Japanese motorbikes, just then arriving in France, were all the rage in school-
yard discussions.) From morning to night
our friend fed us small lies and gross fabri-
cations, brazenly inventing new stories even
when they contradicted preceding ones. An
orphan at 10:00 a.m., an only son at noon, he
could dig up four sisters by midafternoon, one
of them a figure-skating champion. As for
his father—in reality a sober civil servant—he
became, depending on the day, the inventor
of the atom bomb, the Beatles' manager, or

General de Gaulle's unacknowledged son. Since Olivier neglected to give coherence to the dishes he served up, we would have been the last to expect consistency of him. When he came out with some utterly outlandish fable we would voice tentative doubts, but he defended his good faith with such indignant protests of "I swear!" that we would swiftly back down.

When I last checked, Olivier was neither a fighter pilot nor a secret agent nor adviser to an emir (careers he once considered). Fairly predictably, it is in the advertising world that he wields his inexhaustible faculty for gilding every lily.

I should not feel morally superior to Olivier, for today I envy him his mastery of the storyteller's art. I am not sure I will ever acquire such a gift, although I, too, am beginning to forge glorious substitute destinies for myself. I am occasionally a Formula One driver, and you've certainly seen me burning up the track at Monza or Silverstone. That mysterious white racer without a brand name, a number, or commercial advertisements is me. Stretched out on my bed—I mean, in my cockpit—I hurl myself into the corners, my head, weighed down by my helmet, wrenched painfully sideways by gravitational pull. I have also been cast as a soldier in a TV series on history's great battles. I have fought alongside Vercingetorix against Caesar, turned back the invading

Arabs at Poitiers, helped Napoléon to victory, and survived Verdun. Since I have just been wounded in the D-day landings, I cannot swear that I will join the airdrop into Dien Bien Phu. Under the physical therapist's gaze, I am a Tour de France long shot on the verge of pulling off a record-setting victory. Success soothes my aching muscles. I am a phenomenal downhill skier. I can still hear the roar of the crowd on the slope and the singing of the wind in my ears. I was miles ahead of the favorites. I swear!

"A Day in the Life"

Here we come to the end of the road—that disastrous Friday, December 8, 1995. Ever since beginning this book, I have intended to describe my last moments as a perfectly functioning earthling. But I have put it off so long that now, on the brink of this bungee jump into my past, I feel suddenly dizzy. How can I begin to recall those long futile hours, as elusive as drops of mercury from a broken thermometer? How can I describe waking for the last time, heedless, perhaps a little grumpy, beside the lithe, warm body of a tall, dark-haired woman? Everything that day was gray, muted, resigned: the sky, the people, the city, collective nerves on edge after several days of a transport strike. Like millions of Parisians, our eyes empty and our complexions dull, Florence and I embarked like zombies on a new day of punishment amid the indescribable chaos caused by the strike. I mechanically carried out all those simple acts that today seem miraculous to me: shaving, dressing, downing a hot chocolate. Weeks earlier, I had chosen this day to test the latest model of a German automobile: the importer had put a car and driver at my disposal for the whole day. At the appointed hour, a most businesslike young man was waiting outside, leaning against a gunmetal-gray BMW. Through the apartment window I eyed the big sedan, solid and sleek. I wondered how my old Levi's jacket would look in so sophisticated a vehicle. I pressed my forehead against the windowpane to gauge the temperature outside. Florence softly stroked the nape of my neck. Our farewells were brief, our lips scarcely brushing together. I am already running down stairs that smell of floor polish. It will be the last of the smells of my past.

I read the news today, oh boy...

Between crisis-fraught traffic reports, the radio plays a Beatles song, "A Day in the Life." Crossing the Bois de Boulogne, the BMW glides like a flying carpet, a private world of luxury and comfort. My driver is pleasant. I tell him of my plans for the afternoon: to pick up my son from his mother's place, twenty-five miles outside Paris, and bring him back to the city in early evening.

He didn't notice that the lights had changed...

Théophile and I have not had a heart-to-heart talk, a man-to-man exchange, since I moved out of the family home in July. I plan to take him to the theater to see the new Philippe Arias play, then to eat oysters at a restaurant on Place Clichy. It's all set: we are spending the weekend together. I only hope the strike will not frustrate our plans.

I'd love to turn you on...

I love the arrangement of this number, in which the whole orchestra reaches a crescendo and holds it until the explosion of the final note. Like a piano crashing down seven floors. We reach Levallois. The BMW stops outside my office, and I arrange to meet the driver at 3:00 p.m.

There is only one message on my desk, but what a message! I have to put in an immediate return call to Simone V., former minister for health, once the most popular woman in France, tenured for life at the top spot on the magazine's imaginary honor roll. Since this kind of call is rare, I first ask around to find what we might have said or done to provoke this quasi-divine personality. "I think she's unhappy with her photo in our last issue," my assistant tactfully suggests. I skim through the issue and reach the offending photo, a montage that ridicules rather than glorifies our idol. It is one of the mysteries of our trade. You work for weeks on a subject, it goes back and forth among the most skillful pairs of hands, and no one spots the glaring blunder that a neophyte would spot in a second. I am pitched into an authentic long-distance tornado. She is convinced that the magazine has been plotting against her for years, so I have the greatest difficulty persuading her that, on the contrary, she is a cult figure at *Elle*. Normally such damage control is the job of production chief

Anne-Marie, who handles all celebrities with kid gloves, whereas as a diplomat I am more akin to Tintin's friend Captain Haddock than to Henry Kissinger. When we hang up after a forty-five-minute exchange, I feel exactly like a trampled doormat.

Although the editorial staff likes to dismiss our chief's luncheons as "rather a bore," they wouldn't miss them for anything in the world. Our boss, known variously to his supporters as Geronimo, Louis XI, and the Ayatollah, regularly hosts luncheons in order to "take stock," as he puts it. It is here on the top floor of the magazine, in the biggest executive dining room, that our generalissimo offers his subjects clues about where they stand in his affections. His remarks range from praise couched in velvet tones to the most lacerating of rebukes, and he possesses a whole repertoire of gestures, scowls, and beard scratchings, which over the years we have learned to decipher. Of that final meal I remember very little, except that the condemned man's last drink was water. I think the main course was beef. Perhaps we all caught mad cow disease, which nobody at that time talked about. Since it incubates for fifteen years, we still have time left. The only illness reported that day was President Mitterrand's. The whole of Paris had been hanging on his medical reports, wondering whether he would last the weekend. As it turned out, he had another whole month to live. The worst thing about these lunches is that they go on forever. To save time, I sneaked out afterward through my office, without saying goodbye to anyone. When I met my driver, evening was already falling on the glass facades. It was well past four.

"We're going to be caught in this mess, sir."

"I'm truly sorry—"

"It's you I'm thinking about, sir."

For a second I feel like chucking the whole thing: canceling the theater, postponing my weekend with Théophile, retreating to my bed with a plate of cheese and the crossword puzzle. I decide to fight this sense of utter exhaustion that has come over me.

"We'll just have to avoid the freeway."

"Whatever you think..."

Despite its power, the BMW bogs down in the traffic milling on the Pont de Suresnes. We drive past the Saint-Cloud racecourse and then the Raymond-Poincaré Hospital at Garches. I cannot pass this spot without recalling a quite sinister childhood episode. When I was at the Lycée Condorcet, a gym teacher used to take us to the Marche Stadium at Vaucresson for outdoor sports of the kind I detested. One day our bus ran smack into a man who had dashed out of the hospital without looking where he was going. There was a strange noise, the sound of brakes, and the man died instantly, leaving a bloody streak along the bus windows. It was a winter afternoon, like today. By the time the police finished asking questions, it was evening. A different driver took us back to Paris. At the rear of the bus they were singing "Penny Lane" in shaky voices. Still the Beatles. What songs will Théophile remember when he is forty-four?

After an hour and a half of driving, we reach our goal, the house where I spent ten years of my life. Fog hangs over the garden, which once rang with so many yells and so much helpless, happy laughter. Théophile is waiting for us at the gate, sitting on his backpack, ready for the weekend. I would have liked to phone Florence, my new girlfriend, but it is Friday and she is at her parents' place for the Sabbath. I expect to speak to her after the play. Only once have I participated in that Jewish ritual—here at Montainville, in the house of the old Tunisian doctor who brought my children into the world.

From this point onward, everything becomes blurred. Nevertheless, I get behind the wheel of the BMW, focusing on the orange-tinted dashboard lights. I am functioning in slow motion, and in the beam of the headlights I barely recognize turns I have negotiated several thousand times. I feel sweat beading my forehead, and when I overtake a car I see it double. At the first intersection, I pull over. I stagger from the BMW, almost unable to stand upright, and collapse on the rear seat. I have one idea in my head: to get back to the village and to the home of my sister-in-law Diane, a nurse. Half conscious, I ask Théophile to run and get her as soon as we reach her house. A few seconds later, Diane is there. Her decision is swift. "We have to get to the clinic. As quickly as we can." It is ten miles away. This time, the driver tears off grand-prix style. I feel extremely strange, as if I had swallowed an LSD tablet, and I reflect that I am too old for such fantasies. Not for a second does it occur to me that I may be dying. On the road to Mantes, the BMW purrs along at top speed and we overtake a long line of cars, honking insistently to force our way through. I try to say something like "Slow down. I'll get better. It's not worth risking an accident." But no sound comes from my mouth, and my head, no longer under my control, wobbles on my neck. The Beatles and their song of this morning come back into my memory. *And though the news was rather sad . . . I saw the photograph.* In no time we are at the clinic. People are running frantically about. I am transferred, limp and sprawling, into a wheelchair. The BMW's doors click softly shut. Someone once told me that you can tell a good car by the quality of that click. I am dazzled by the neon lighting in the corridor. In the elevator, strangers heap encouragement upon me, and the Beatles launch into the finale of "A Day in the Life." The piano crashing down from the seventh floor. Before it hits the ground, I have time for one last thought: We'll have to cancel the play. We would have been late in any case. We'll go tomorrow night. Where could Théophile have got to? And then I sink into a coma.

Season of Renewal

Summer is nearly over. The nights grow chilly, and once again I am snuggled beneath thick blue blankets stamped "Paris Hospitals." Each day brings its assortment of familiar faces: linen maid, dentist, mailman, a nurse who has just had a grandson, and the man who last June broke his finger on a bed rail. I rediscover old landmarks, old habits; and this, the start of my first autumn season at the hospital, has made one thing very plain—I have indeed begun a new life, and that life is here, in this bed, that wheelchair, and those corridors. Nowhere else.

September means the end of vacations, it means back to school and to work, and here at the hospital it's time to start a new season. I've made some progress. I can now grunt the little song about the kangaroo, musical testimony to my progress in speech therapy:

The Kangaroo escaped the zoo.
"Goodbye zoo!" cried Kangaroo...
Cleared the wall with one clean jump,
Leaped across with a great big thump...

But here at Berck I hear only the faintest echoes of the outside world's collective return to work and responsibility... its return to the world of literature and journalism and school, to the workaday world of Paris. I shall hear more about it soon, when my friends start journeying back to Berck with their summer's worth of news. It seems that Théophile now goes around in sneakers whose heels light up every time he takes a step. You can follow him in the dark. Meanwhile, I am savoring this last week of August with a heart that is almost light, because for the first time in a long while I don't have that awful sense of a countdown—the feeling triggered at the beginning of a vacation that inevitably spoils a good part of it.

Her elbows on the small mobile Formica table that serves as her desk, Claude is reading out these pages we have patiently extracted from the void every afternoon for the last two months. Some pages I am pleased to see again. Others are disappointing. Do they add up to a book? As I listen to Claude, I study her dark hair, her very pale cheeks, which sun and wind have scarcely touched with pink, the long bluish veins on her hands, and the articles scattered about the room. I will put them in my mind's scrapbook as reminders of a summer of hard work. The big blue notebook whose pages she fills with her neat, formal handwriting; the pencil case like the ones schoolchildren use, full of spare ballpoints; the heap of paper napkins ready for my worst coughing-and-spitting fits; and the red raffia purse in which she periodically rummages for coins for the coffee machine. Her purse is half open, and I see a hotel room key, a metro ticket, and a hundred-franc note folded in four, like objects brought back by a space probe sent to earth to study how earthlings live, travel, and trade with one another. The sight leaves me pensive and confused. Does the cosmos contain keys for opening up my diving bell? A subway line with no terminus? A currency strong enough to buy my freedom back? We must keep looking. I'll be off now.

Berck-Plage, July–August 1996

If you have enjoyed reading this large print book and you would like more information on how to order a Wheeler Large Print Book, please write to:

Wheeler Publishing, Inc.
P.O. Box 531
Accord, MA 02018-0531